Essays on Order, Book 3

The Third Collection of Essays

Book 1 consisted of essays designed to engage the reader in self-awareness and an awareness of the order and chaos that surrounds us all. Book 2 was to take the reader one step deeper into what order can do and what chaos cannot, revelation. Book 3 will take the reader to the next step of order, understanding. Understanding why things are the way they are and what you as the reader can do to apply order to these various circumstances. Book 3 promises to be quite challenging as the reader moves through the essays.

As in Books 1 and 2, you should try not to read all the essays in a single reading. I suggest you read one essay, think about it, re-read it, and then re-think it before moving to the next essay. In this manner you will absorb more of the idea than just the content. This is simply an ordered approach for you to read the Essays on Order, good luck and enjoy the essays.

www.essaysonorder.com

Chuck Pyburn

Essays on Order

The Third Collection of Essays

Book 3 – Table of Contents

1. An Essay on Order – The Final Option, Suicide
2. An Essay on Order – The Convict
3. An Essay on Order – Imminent Domain
4. An Essay on Order – The Shortcut
5. An Essay on Order – Secrets
6. An Essay on Order – Motivation
7. An Essay on Order – The Oath
8. An Essay on Order – Loyalty and Obedience
9. An Essay on Order – Revenge
10. An Essay on Order – Justice
11. An Essay on Order – Greed
12. An Essay on Order – Corruption
13. An Essay on Order – Law
14. An Essay on Order – Crossing Over
15. An Essay on Order – B Minor
16. An Essay on Order – Freedom
17. An Essay on Order – Liberty
18. An Essay on Order – Economics
19. An Essay on Order – Opportunity
20. An Essay on Order – Truth

An Essay on Order – The Final Option, Suicide

In the darkest corners of our mind is where we keep the final option. I've seen this option played out several times in my life, with it always having the same results. This essay is one the hardest I've written so far, the memories are as fresh today as when I first obtained them. Here is my take on the final option.

The Essay

All of life's emotions are scaled from low to high and in the case of the final option, the thought and deed of suicide is rated both lowest and highest on this scale. It is regarded as the final option since, if executed correctly, there are no subsequent options. There are no other emotions, and or deeds, that occupy both ends of the emotional spectrum simultaneously. It should also be noted that the final option is considered the most extreme condition in chaos and can be the highest of ordered thoughts and deeds. With such a vagarious discrepancy between considerations, the conclusive conduct of the final option will remain with why the act was perpetrated and its subsequent consequences. Notwithstanding, the mental and physical conditions preceding the execution of the final option must also be considered.

The physical condition of an individual committing the final option will either be perfectly healthy or they are suffering a debilitating disease or physical impairment. In the case of the latter, the final option is seen as a release from an inevitable conclusion. In the case of an individual being perfectly healthy, the individual must either be emotionally depraved or thoughtfully single-minded when executing the final option. To be emotionally depraved the individual will have been subjected to a circumstance to which they have concluded there is no possibility of returning to the population. In all cases it will be true that, the basic four needs of life (water, food, shelter and companionship) no longer have any meaning for the individual committing the final option. If it is the case that the individual is thoughtfully single-minded then it must also be the case that the deed is the result of service to the population. This will be the rare occurrence to which an ordered person is called upon for the good of another or for the good of the population. It will always be the case that when an ordered person engages in a lethal activity to save another that they do so with full knowledge of the consequences. Committing the final option when in service to the population offers no higher regard.

The method used to commit the final option is not relevant as the potential means are limitless. It is sufficient in that an individual will use the most expeditious and lethal means available.

The consequences of committing the final option are ubiquitous with the only exception being service. The most immediate consequence of the final option is that the individual was successful in removing themselves from the population and their immediate family. Their failings are no longer of any concern but what is of concern are the responsibilities and societal placement of the individual. Each of these areas will now have to be assumed by other family members or by the population.

As we are all offspring, we all share the commonality in that our life was not of our choosing. The decision that allows us to enjoy life was the decision made by our parents and on it goes throughout our ancestry. While the decision to live was not ours, the responsibility to live is ours and as such, its untimely forfeiture must result in penalty. The penalty will not be paid by the person committing the final option but by those that survive the person. The penalty paid by the survivors can be property, emotional and family stability or placement within the population. The penalties by the survivors may be one or all of the aforementioned penalties but there will be a penalty. In the case of exercising the final option as the result of service, there will never be a penalty. When it is the case that the loss is service related, the responsibilities left vacant will gladly be assumed by family and population.

It should also be noted that the memory of an individual that exercised the final option will not live passed the next generation. The memory of the individual will be purged from existence as quickly as time and circumstance will allow. The memory of a service related exercise of the final option will be memorialized.

At the extreme end of chaos there is suicide and at the extreme reaches of order there is sacrifice. Between these two extremes exists the responsibility to live to our fullest potential, ever mindful that our life was a gift. A gift we should never try to return.

Chuck Pyburn

An Essay on Order – The Convict

A lot of us have gone to jail at one time or another and for various reasons. The problem is not in going to jail but what happens while we are in jail. This essay is my take on what the convict doesn't know.

The Essay

Why a person is incarcerated is not as important as what occurs without that person's involvement. There are three aspects to be considered in this discussion. The first aspect will be the individual, the second aspect will be the family of the incarcerated person and the final aspect will be the professional consideration of the person having been incarcerated. It should be noted that these discussion assume that that the individual has been rightfully incarcerated for a violation of current statutes as established by the existing government.

No one individual is born to be imprisoned. It will always be the case that the individual has made the decision to commit a crime that warrants imprisonment. It will also, always, be the case that every individual is born to fulfill a destiny that does not include imprisonment. It then must also be the case that when a person is imprisoned that their destiny will be unfulfilled and their contributions to the population will never exist. It may be the case that when an individual is released from imprisonment that they begin their life anew, but their original destiny will never be realized. Therefore, it will always be the case that when a person has been imprisoned that they will never be the person they were meant to be. The person, the life, the contributions of a person released from prison will never be what they should have been.

The family of an imprisoned individual will be suffering the loss of that person's participation, in whatever capacity that participation existed. The family will have to adapt in order to compensate for the lost participation of the imprisoned individual. These compensatory efforts will build a resentment that can never be undone. While it can never be the case that the imprisoned individual will be completely removed from the family, it will always be the case that the imprisoned individual will never be a complete family member. It will also be the case that the imprisoned individual will never fully re-assume the participatory responsibilities they once enjoyed.

The professional aspirations of an incarcerated individual cease when they become incarcerated. While they cannot loose their expertise they will loose the experience they would have gotten had they not been incarcerated. Along with the loss of experience will be the trust of the professional community towards any future conduct in that professional capacity. It will then be the case that if the incarcerated individual is released, then their contributions to the population will be a mere derivative of what they should have been.

    Order demands that a population comply with the laws as approved by the population. If it is the case that a law has no merit then it should also be the case that the population removes that law. If, through an act of chaos, an individual perpetrates an act contrary to the accepted laws of a population then the resulting incarceration is rightful and this essay will be played out.

Chuck Pyburn

An Essay on Order – Imminent Domain

When I was a kid I read about how in the old days only landowners could vote. I made up my mind right then to one day become a landowner. If I'd only known then, what I know now.

The Essay

Imminent domain has existed since the beginnings of domains, kingdoms, territories and the like. The practice has remained consistent even though the names of the participating population have changed. The state, or whatever form of government is in power, owns the land and allows its tenant population to purchase a parcel of the land. The tenant has control of the land so long as the tenant pays taxes to the owner, fights the states wars and provided services to the state as required. If any of the three previous conditions are not met then the state will simply resume control of the land.

In the case of the state taxing the tenant, the state may tax the purchase of the land and will require subsequent annual taxes for as long as the tenant has control of the land. Through this taxation the state declares its imminent ownership of the land and through paying taxes the tenant agrees to acquiesce. The tenant may will the land to their heir but, the taxation will never end so long as the state does not exercise control of the land.

In the case of fighting the states wars, the tenant population will provide to the state those able bodied personnel the state requires to fight in the war of their choosing. The tenant population will either volunteer or be conscripted so long as they live on the land. Only the state may release a member of the population back to the tenant from which they came.

In the case of providing services to the state, the tenant population will provide to the state those members of the population required by the state to conduct the business of the state. The administration and enforcement of the state with regard to the tenant population will be the occupations of these acquired tenants.

It will also be the case that the state may at any time, through condemnation or seizure, retake the land with or without notice and with or without compensation to the tenant.

In the oldest of days, a tenant would have to have permission from the state to hunt the wildlife that occupied the land. The consideration was such that whoever owned the land, owned whatever was on the land.

It should also be noted that there are no religious texts in conflict with imminent domain. In all cases there is a division between the conduct of a religion and the conduct of the state. And lastly, only those people that are alive and cognizant have any preference regarding imminent domain.

In the division between order and chaos lies the condition of imminent domain. Without such privilege there would only be the chaos of anarchy, the strong surviving over the weak. If therefore becomes the case that if imminent domain is applied fairly and equitably then order may prevail. If it becomes the case that imminent domain is applied harshly and without grievance, then where there was order there will now be chaos and a population will not strive in chaos.

Chuck Pyburn

An Essay on Order – The Shortcut

It occurred to me at a very young age that there was no easy way to get stuff. Back in those days, my brothers and I would walk the highway after school looking for coke bottles. You could get two cents apiece for them back then, a lot of money for a kid. Now, every time I see somebody looking for the easy road I still just laugh to myself.

The Essay

With every intention there are elements that allow the intention to be for good or for bad. These elements are always the deciding factors as the intention moves from conception to final result. And the final result will either demonstrate order or it will demonstrate chaos but it cannot demonstrate both.

When it is the case that an individual conceives of an idea that will inevitably improve their lot in life, then it will be the case that the individual will act on that intention. The idea itself will always be in regard to affluence or position within the population. Affluence will always be the easier of the intentions to conceive and act upon and will, therefore, be the first idea. It will always be the case that those that achieve affluence, by using a shortcut, will have contempt for those that do not have affluence.

The shortcut is the key that defines whether or not the result of the intention will be in order or in chaos. If the result is achieved ahead of its time then it will always be the case that the result is in chaos. If the result is achieved as a natural occurrence of consistent and straightforward action then it will always be the case that the result is in order.

With regard to position within the population, it will always be the case that position is achieved in one of two fashions, it will either be sought after or it will occur as a natural progression of demonstrated leadership. When it is the case that a position within the population is sought then it will always be the case that the person is not prepared for that position. The ability to properly manage a position requires the experience and seasoning that naturally prepares an individual for that position. To circumvent the preparation aspect of a position is to guarantee a chaotic execution of that position. Those that achieve position as a natural occurrence of their ability are grounded in order and will not allow a misuse of that position.

It will always be the case that those that are in order will care little about affluence or position within the population. The ordered person understands that affluence and position will occur as a natural result of every day attention to honesty and integrity. To do more is simply, not possible.

Chuck Pyburn

An Essay on Order – Secrets

It's hard to go through life without making mistakes of one kind or another. It's equally difficult in the professional arena to not know things that by their nature must be kept secret. The question then becomes the costs associated with keeping secrets. This is my take on secrets.

The Essay

There are only two varieties of secrets, personal or professional. Regardless of the variety, the ordered aspect of a secret is in keeping it a secret. The chaos of a secret is in the telling.

In regards to personal secrets, a personal secret will always be an action that was either done to the individual or an action that was done by the individual. In either case, the committed action was unpleasant enough that it does not warrant discussion. It will also be the case that the action was only deemed unpleasant after the action had occurred. Prior to the action occurring, the action was deemed appropriate. It will also be the case that the individual did survive the action. And lastly, it must also be the case that had the individual thought through the action, that the action would either have not been committed or that the individual would not have allowed themselves to be the recipient of the action. Now that the action has occurred and the individual did survive the action, and the action has been deemed unpleasant, the action is now a secret to the individual in that it is not discussed.

There is only one type of professional secret and that secret is the direction to not disseminate information. The nature of the profession and the corresponding actions required in the conduct of that profession are not relevant to the secret, only disseminating the information surrounding the professional action is secret. The action is not secret to those involved or responsible for the direction of the professional action.

By reserving personal and professional information the individual has declared that there are boundaries within their mind that will prohibit open discussion of this reserved information. As such, this reserved information will never be purged from that individual's mind prior to their expiration. Professional information will seldom be reserved in that the secretive information may be discussed with other members of the action or those responsible for the action. Personal secrets are of no physical threat to the individual in that they did survive the action. Notwithstanding, by not being able to discuss the reserved information, the individual is destined to actively remember the secretive action.

      Order demands that professional secrets by kept against all odds. Order equally demands that personal secrets be discussed, preferably with a professional, so that the individual may purge the secret from active memory. To release professional secrets is to invite chaos into an action that has already occurred. To maintain personal secrets is to maintain chaos within that reserved section of the mind that otherwise would be available for new information.

Chuck Pyburn

An Essay on Order – Motivation

Going from the Marine Corps Recon to Army Special Forces was quite a culture shock for me. In training for Special Forces all I heard people talk about was staying motivated and I didn't have a clue what they were talking about. In my world, doing the work of training was just another day at the office.

The Essay

Motivation is a mid level life emotion that is strictly reserved for those members of the population that are in chaos. For one to be motivated it must first be the case that the individual was not motivated. It then becomes the case that motivation is the temporary reconditioning of a chaotic individual in order to exceed what the chaotic person would deem as appropriate in that to not do so would put their four basic needs of life, in part or in whole, in threat or jeopardy. The four basic needs of life are; water, food, shelter and companionship. It must also be the case that the chaotic individual believes the threat of loss to be real and substantive. For the chaotic individual to believe the threat was not real and substantive would cause them to not be motivated, regardless. It will also be the case that the chaotic individual will only be motivated so long as the threat exists. Without the threat, the chaotic individual will return to the behavior they have considered as appropriate.

An ordered individual cannot be motivated. An ordered individual will routinely work to exceed their own expectations. Additionally, the ordered individual is grounded in honesty and integrity and as such, they cannot do more. The ordered individual will consistently look for newer and better ways to accomplish whatever manner of task is given them. It is also the case that an ordered individual has successfully secured their basic four needs of life and, as such, they cannot be put in threat or jeopardy.

Chuck Pyburn

An Essay on Order – The Oath

Over my life time I've taken many oaths. All of them were required before I could do the job and of course, I meant every word every time. Many people take an oath but few really understand them. This is my take on the subject.

The Essay

Over the centuries, ruling bodies have used many tactics to control their population and enforce their will on that population and neighboring populations. One such tactic is taking an oath. It will always be the case that an oath will require consequences if not upheld and only the ruling body will require an oath. The oath will be a swearing by the individual to fully comply with the wishes of the ruling body. The oath will be composed by the ruling body and will compel the individual to conform to the wishes of the ruling body. Only the ruling body will dictate the consequences if the oath is not complied with. All other oaths, regardless of intent, do not carry the burden of consequence as do those of the ruling body. Of all of the possible professions that do take an oath, only two have consequences. The first oath with consequence is in giving testimony to the ruling body. The second oath with consequence is in providing enforcement for the ruling body.

Jurisprudence will demand that an individual take an oath prior to giving testimony. By requiring an oath, the individual is then subject to penalty if found to be untruthful. By so requiring, the laws of that ruling body compel an individual to subject their liberties and freedoms to possible forfeiture if it is determined that their testimony is considered false. The purpose of this oath is to compel an individual to speak the truth less they suffer the consequences.

Prior to enforcing the will of the ruling body, the ruling body will require the individual to take an oath to enforce the will of the ruling body. By taking an oath to enforce, the individual has agreed to subject themselves to a second set of jurisprudence that specifically addresses that group of enforcement. The purpose of this oath is obedience in enforcing the will of the ruling body less the individual suffer the consequences of disobedience.

It should also be noted that only the ruling body may release an individual from their oath.

An ordered person would comply with the oath so long as it did not conflict with their sense of morality. If it was the case that an ordered person did act contrary to the oath then they would do their utmost to mitigate the consequences but they would not compromise their integrity. A person in chaos would comply with the oath so long as it was advantageous to comply, regardless of personal consequence. Lastly, an oath is serious in that what one may be asked to do could easily be contrary to what one may find acceptable.

Chuck Pyburn

An Essay on Order – Loyalty and Obedience

Having been in the military I learned of these two areas but it took some time to understand. Now that I understand it is my hope is to pass that understanding on to the reader.

The Essay

Obedience is one of the few vertical attitudes within a given population. Obedience will only be in the regard to do something or in the regard to not do something. One may not be commanded to think, or not think, something. It will always be the case that an individual is either obeying another person or thing or the individual is causing another individual to obey them or they are creating a thing that must be obeyed. Obedience is also positional within a population. The more command one, or the thing, has within a population then the more of that population will have to obey. Lastly, for a command to be obeyed it must also be the case that there is a consequence for not obeying. A consequence will, in all cases, be a negative effect on an individual's four basic needs of life which are; water, food, shelter and companionship. It will never be the case that failing to obey will not have a negative effect on that person's basic four needs of life, in part or in total.

An ordered person will choose to obey a command either because of the rightness of the command or because the ordered person does not have the wherewithal to counter the command. An ordered person will never obey a command simply because of the person giving the command. An ordered person will never obey a command that is counter to their morality or integrity. If an ordered person does not agree with the command, but does comply with the command, then it will be the case that the ordered person will work to change the structure that allows the issuance of the command.

A person in chaos will obey a command because they fear the threat to their basic four needs of life. A person in chaos will obey a command regardless of the personal compromise. A person in chaos will only see the person that is giving the command and will never see the position that is giving the command. And lastly, a person in chaos will never challenge a command.

Loyalty is one of the few horizontal attitudes within a population. Loyalty is the combined determination to complete a task within a specific situation. Loyalty is always situational in that loyalty will only exist so long as the situation exists. It will also be the case that loyalty will only exist for the members of that situation and only for as long as they are active members of that situation. And it will always be the case that loyalty within a situation is pervasive to all members of the situation regardless of position within the situation. It will always be the case that only the ordered members of a situation are loyal, those that are in chaos are merely being obedient to the commands required by the situation.

Chuck Pyburn

An Essay on Order – Revenge

I got into my first fight on the first day of the first grade so I learned early about revenge. Luckily, as I grew older I was able to think through it as I hope you will. This is my take on revenge.

The Essay

Revenge is the chaotic desire of an individual to inflict as much, or greater, wrongdoing on the person or peoples that inflicted wrongdoing upon the individual. It is interesting to note that since revenge cannot be learned it must also be the case that revenge cannot be taught which, therefore, makes revenge the spontaneous result of a wrongdoing. It will also always be the case that revenge, regardless of any additional participants, is individual in nature in that only the wronged individual is seeking revenge. It will also be the case that the individual is seeking recompense for damage, in part or in total, to their basic four needs of life which are water, food, shelter and companionship. And it will always be the case that once an individual has committed an act of revenge that the act cannot be undone. Lastly, regardless of the quality, or quantity, of the act of revenge, it will never be the case that the wrong suffered by the individual shall be made right.

Chuck Pyburn

An Essay on Order – Justice

Early on I had a tough time differentiating between justice and revenge but once I figured it out I was able to really begin to accomplish the better parts of life. I hope this works for you like it worked for me.

The Essay

Justice is the ordered attempt at making a wrongdoing right. A wrongdoing will always be damage to an individual's basic four needs of life which are water, food, shelter and companionship. Since it will never be the case that an act of wrongdoing can be undone, it will be the case that the perpetrator of the wrongdoing be held accountable for the action and prevented from committing a similar act of wrongdoing. Justice may only be carried out by those individuals appointed by the state to conduct such enforcement without bias and without attachment.

It will never be the case that the individual that suffered the wrongful act will receive justice. Justice may only be imposed on the perpetrator of the wrongful act. The individual that suffered the wrongful act may only enjoy that justice has, or has not, been meted.

An ordered individual will safeguard against wrongdoing while only an individual in chaos may contemplate a wrongdoing. Safeguarding against a wrongdoing will always minimize the possibility of a wrongdoing but it will never discount the potential of wrongdoing.

It will always be the case that the threat of wrongdoing will be ever present just as the threat of justice against the perpetrators is ever present. Justice demands that the ordered be vigilant and the ordered demand that justice be relentless.

Chuck Pyburn

An Essay on Order – Greed

Growing up poor you learn early on about the have and the have not's. Your choices are to remain one of the have not's or to get off your butt and do something about it. It never occurred to me that I could blame somebody else for my condition. This is my take on greed.

The Essay

Greed is one of the few attitudes of chaos that are singular in direction in that it only points to those that are not in chaos. For a person to not be in chaos it must be the case that they have secured their four basic needs of life which are water, food, shelter and companionship. It must also be the case that an ordered person has acquired their four basic of needs of life to such an extent that they are not in threat of losing those needs. Greed then becomes the attitude that the success of the ordered should be given to those that cannot secure their four basic needs of life or to those that are in chaos.

Successful acquisition of the four basic needs of life can never be given as each acquisition is the result of the individual's effort to live a successful life. If it is the case that the individual does not engage life towards obtaining these acquisitions then it will also be the case that the individual will not have the wherewithal to enjoy and maintain these acquisitions.

Lastly, those that are in chaos may easily be desirous of the success of those that are in order but it will never be the case that those that are in chaos will acquire the success of those that are in order, regardless. It finally becomes the case that the success of the ordered may allow for generosity but it will never, nor could it possibly ever, be the case that ability be transferred to inability.

Chuck Pyburn

An Essay on Order – Corruption

This is a tough topic in that it took me years to figure out what it meant and what impact it could have. Of all the topics this one is the more dangerous, enjoy the essay.

The Essay

Corruption is quite simply the denial of services to the population for what is to be considered as personal gain. Corruption will only exist in agencies supported by the state. Corruption will never occur in business or in the life of an individual or in the life of a population. It will always be the case that whatever illicit gains an agent of the state may have derived from such activity that it will not be sustained or remembered. It shall also be the case that the denied services to the population will occur as they are mandated by the population. It will also be the case that the ordered agents of the state will exact a penalty of those agents of the state that are engaged in such an activity.

Chuck Pyburn

An Essay on Order – Law

I can't count the laws I've broken over a lifetime. The laws I've broken range from kidnapping (accused by the way, she was seventeen) to simple speeding. I've never done any hard time, unlike one of my brothers, but I have spent a night or two in the pokey and in various countries. When you know what law is it is not that difficult to stay out of trouble.

The Essay

The first purpose of law is to determine the least conduct that is acceptable to the population. The second purpose of law is to determine the least conduct that is acceptable to the state. The difference between these two determinations is in objective. The first determination is to facilitate the interaction between those that are in chaos and the ordered that need no laws. The second determination is to define what freedoms may not exist for the population. There can only be two categories of law, those that sustain the basic four acquisitions of life, or the ordered laws, and those that regulate life, or the laws that offer consequence above choice. The basic four needs of life are water, food, shelter and companionship. The ordered laws are universal while the regulatory laws are regionally specific.

The ordered laws are universal in that they apply equally to all of mankind and cannot be denied. These laws protect, defend and maintain that all individuals are able to seek their basic four needs of life.

While the regulatory laws deny freedom they do also fall into two categories, those that protect and those that deny. The regulatory laws that protect the population from abuses may, at some point, be applied unilaterally whereas the laws that are regional laws may be dismissed.

When it is the case that a law offers consequence above order then the law will be disobeyed. When it is the case that the law offers order above consequence then that law will be obeyed.

Law can never condemn the birthright to live and pursue the basic four needs of life. Law can never condemn the population moving forward. Law will establish the minimum level of interaction between those that are in chaos and those that are in order. Be aware that the law will never apply to those that are in order for they need no law.

Chuck Pyburn

An Essay on Order – Crossing Over

One night, about a hundred years ago or so it seems, I was in a bar trying to score some chicks when I saw this one dude. At the time I was running with a biker gang and the word was out, "if you see this guy, do him justice". I bided my time drinking draft beer until he finally made his move to the bathroom. I followed him in with my Buck 110 in hand. As he stood there relieving himself I made my decision. I put my knife away and walked out, and kept on walking.

The Essay

As in all processes there comes a time to evaluate the process. One ponders if this process is going in the desired direction? And again, have all of the necessary steps been taken in the process to ensure the objective? And lastly, is it time to take stop this process and begin a new process? As the people are born to order and then learn chaos, so too must it be true that a person in chaos must learn what order is and how to live it.

Order begins when a person understands the importance of the basic four needs of life which are water, food, shelter and companionship. It is true that a person in chaos may acquire these four aspects of life but a person in chaos will never understand their intrinsic value.

Understanding water is the difference between needing water and having water in a never ending supply. When it is the case that a person needs water then it is also the case that the individual cannot readily supply themselves with water, hence they are in chaos. When it is the case that a person in chaos has a temporary supply of water then it will also be the case that that person will be temporarily in order with regards to the acquisition of water. This same argument will hold true for food and for shelter but not for companionship. Suffice it to say that, being able to temporarily acquire three of the basic four needs to life will allow an individual in chaos to make correct choices from time to time or when they are temporarily in order.

It will also be the case that as an individual matures they will develop the necessary personal skills to interact with other members of the population. An individual will maintain these skills if it is the case that these skills will serve them when either temporarily in chaos or when temporarily in order. These tested skills along with their capacity for intelligence will determine an individual's success in life. Success being measured against one's ability to acquire the basic four needs of life and not having those needs put in threat. If it is the case that an individual remains in and out of chaos their entire life then these skills will never be altered as they are known by the individual to be tested and true. If it is the case that the individual has made the decision to live in order then these skills, in their entirety, will not serve the individual. It will be the case that those tested skills that do serve the individual in order will be maintained while those tested skills that do not serve the ordered individual will be discarded. The discarded skills will be replaced with newly learned skills until once again the individual is assured in their ability to acquire and maintain the basic four needs of life.

With regard to companionship, an individual that is in and out of chaos and order will never know the intrinsic value of the relationship with their companion. They may know the value of their companion but will never know the value of their relationship. Couples in this scenario will either separate and return to the population or remain together as the greater of the remaining poorer choices. It will always be the case that only the ordered may know the relationship with as much intensity as they know their companion. And again, it may only be the case that the companion will reciprocate to the individual when the companion is also in order.

Crossing over at this point becomes the decision of an individual to live in order. Order may be implied or it may simply be the conscious desire to choose the most correct action. Order may also be taught and conversely, order may be learned but it will only be the case that there is order when, and only when, an individual lives in order. For an individual to learn and enjoy the higher, more fulfilling, emotions and attitudes then it must be the case that the individual has decided to live in order.

Chuck Pyburn

An Essay on Order – B Minor

Coming from a long line of wannabe guitar pickers, I learned how to play the guitar fairly early. And as you come up in music you learn about notes and chords. It took a few years but I finally figured out that the saddest note in all of music is B minor.

The Essay

Silent suffering is the worst condition that can be imposed on a population by those that are in chaos. Silent suffering is not caused by disease or illness. Silent suffering does not speak strictly about unfortunate children although they are involved. Silent suffering occurs in a population when a stronger state is in conflict with a weaker state. This conflict causes the population of the weaker state to be denied state services and places them in direct jeopardy as the stronger state overruns the weaker state.

When it is the case that a population is in the state of silent suffering then it must also be the case that there are none to hear their plea's of regress. The population must simply endure until the conflict is resolved.

It will always be the case that the business of the state will never be a concern to the population so long as services are provided. It will only be the case that the population is concerned when it becomes the case that the population is called upon to enforce the will of the state or the population must endure the failings of the state.

As one considers what populations have gone through, are going through and will go through, it then becomes apparent that the note of B minor is the least desirable sound to the ears of the effected population. B minor will be the first note heard by those that are in order and the last note heard by those that are in chaos.

It then must be the case that life begins with the note of A and ends with the note of G. The music that is representative of life must, therefore, be inclusive between the notes of A and G. It must therefore be the case that as one enjoys music that whenever the note B minor is heard, that the voice of the enduring is also heard, there can be no other sound so representing.

Chuck Pyburn

An Essay on Order – Freedom

I've heard folks talk about freedom since I was a kid. We have freedom to do this and we have freedom to do that and I never really heard what freedom is. I've talked to folks when I was in the military about what is freedom and I've talked to folks when I was in college and I'm still waiting for someone to let me know. Meanwhile, this determination of freedom has been around since the beginning and I thought it might need re-telling. Keep in mind when reading the essay that freedom is not a feeling, an attitude or an emotion, it is physically real. Enjoy the essay.

The Essay

There are two categories of freedom, mental and physical. Each category deserves analysis and discussion from the point of origin to the final point of conclusion. Suffice it to say that complete mental freedom occurs at birth and complete physical freedom occurs at death. This essay will contend the limits of freedom between these two extremes and this contention will be applicable for all of mankind.

When an individual is born their mind is only aware of the basic four needs of life which are water, food, shelter and companionship. Their thought processes revolve around these four needs and their countenance will reflect their capacity at acquiring these four needs. It also at this point that, the baby is completely in order with no awareness of chaos, the baby is totally free to consider whatever it wishes. Conversely, it is also at this point that physically, the baby is in complete chaos in that it is totally dependant on its caregivers for the basic four needs of life, without which it would surely die.

As the infant moves into childhood freedom becomes adaptive in that it must allow restrictions with regard to good and bad, with emphasis. It is also at this point that choice is being introduced to the child as well as behavior. With each right selection the child is taught that forgoing that freedom is correct and acting on that specific freedom will incur a consequence. At the child stage the child is beginning to gain physical freedom in that it can begin to control its own bodily functions and move in directions as it sees fit. Even at this point, the child is still totally free to consider whatever it wishes. Order and chaos at this point is still undefined but the child is subjective.

In the adolescent stage the individual is still receiving reinforcement training on right behavior versus wrong behavior or freedom used correctly is rewarded and freedom used incorrectly is with consequence. As the child grows this mental freedom to choose becomes increasingly more restrictive. Meanwhile, as the child grows the physical freedom to do becomes more evident. It is again present that, even at this stage of development the adolescent is still free to consider whatever it wishes. Order and chaos at this stage has still not been identified, explained, or considered.

As the adolescent moves into the teenage years the reinforcement training is lessening as the teenager begins to exercise choice over recommendation. At this point the teenager is beginning to classify consequence and its effect with regard to the basic four needs of life and its socioeconomic impact in everyday life. As well as these considerations, the teenager is also learning about the laws of the state and the acceptable behavior limitations as defined by the population, notwithstanding, the teenager is also learning of the freedom that is impacted by religious choice. Conversely the teenager is also testing the limits and rewards of what is regarded as the correct use of freedom. With every choice the teenager makes the teenager moves between order and chaos. If the teenager determines that the acceptable use of freedom is not that great an award or if the teenager determines that the consequence of what is considered an incorrect use of freedom is not such a detrimental consequence then the teenager is in order in that the teenager is engaging its own thought processes to determine their own direction. Physically, in the teenage state, the teenager is near total physical freedom in that their actions are equally nearing physical order. It should also be noted that in the teenage stage of development the teenager is still dependent for its four basic needs of life but it is, however, free to consider whatever it wishes. At this stage the individual hears suggestions of potential order and chaos but still lacks any definitive input.

As the individual moves into early adulthood the individual will have a rudimentary understanding of which freedoms may be exercised at will and which freedoms will result in consequences ranging from mild to extreme. The individual will also begin to correlate the constraints on freedom by the population, by the state, by the religious and by any other organization the individual may be affiliated with. At the early adulthood stage the individual is at their peak of physical freedom even though they may only exercise that freedom within the confines of the aforementioned freedom restrictions. It will also be at this stage of development that the individual learns of the freedom restrictions imposed by a companion or pending companion and possibly children. It should also be considered that in the early adulthood stage an individual is free to consider whatever it wishes. It is at this stage that the individual feels order and chaos but still lacks intimate knowledge and understanding.

Now the individual has moved into adulthood and has a 'good as it gets' understanding of which freedoms may be exercised at will and which freedoms will result in consequences, and again, ranging from mild to extreme. The individual is aware of their constraints on freedom by the population, by the state, by the religious and by any other organization the individual is affiliated with. At the adulthood stage the individual is past their peak of physical freedom and may only exercise that near perfect physical freedom within the confines of the aforementioned freedom restrictions. It will also be at this stage that physical development has stopped. It should also be considered that in the adulthood stage an individual is free to consider whatever it wishes. It is at this stage that the individual knows there is order and chaos but still lacks the definitions of order and chaos.

Lastly, as the individual moves into late adulthood the individual will have forgotten the understandings of which freedoms may be exercised at will and which freedoms will result in consequences ranging from mild to extreme. At this stage the individual has become routine in their living, strictly accommodating the freedoms lost and not enjoying the remaining freedoms. The individual will also begin to disregard the constraints on freedom by the population, by the state, by the religious and by any other organization the individual may or was affiliated with. In the late adulthood stage caring becomes strictly reserved for family and secondarily for friends. The mental and physical ambitions have simply aged and the realization that the time has come and gone is upon them. It should also be considered that in the late adulthood stage an individual is still free to consider whatever it wishes. It is at this stage that the individual knows there is order and chaos whether they can put a name to it or not.

Understanding that as an individual matures their freedom to act becomes more limited even as their ability to do those actions becomes more capable and all the while they are free to consider whatever they wish. What makes these excursions into the obvious more profound is that the organizations that impede freedom are never at a standstill. As one population grows to accept the loss of a specific freedom by an organization it then becomes the case that the organization become intent on restricting another freedom which in turn will be accepted by the population. When restricted freedom is accepted by the population it then becomes impossible for a single individual to object to the loss of that freedom. The goal of an organization is to control as much of the life wealth and freedom of an individual as it possibly can while still remaining viable to the population.

It then becomes the case that while the freedom of the population decreases then the freedom of those in charge of the organization will increase. It can never be the case that a freedom does not exist but it will always be the case that, without consequence, those that have that freedom may then act upon that freedom. The organization will never penalize the organizer but it will always penalize the organized so long as the organization exists. Throughout all of the organization, and at any time, any one individual is free to consider whatever they wish.

Freedom then becomes the remaining available actions not controlled by the organization; wherein, one is free to do as they wish so long as that freedom is not restricted by the organization. And finally, at the end of an individual's life they are physically free to do whatever they wish even though their mental freedom has been spent. And throughout each of these stages and steps, an individual is free at any time, and anywhere, to consider whatever they wish. A free thought will generate a free action and a free action will always benefit an individual's basic four needs of life and will never harm, impede, or cause an individual to not respect another individual.

Chuck Pyburn

An Essay on Order – Liberty

Having been to numerous countries in the Pacific Basin I've seen firsthand the standards of living and the looks of the people. The 'haves' are few and the 'have not's' are many. All I could do was observe as I was powerless to change their fortune. This essay is a tribute to their struggle.

The Essay

Liberty and freedom cannot coexist within a given population. If it is the case that a population enjoys freedom then it must also be the case that the population is not seeking liberty. When it is the case that the state has encroached on that freedom to the point that the population is no longer able to acquire their basic four needs of life then it will always be the case that the population will react. *The basic four needs of life are water, food, shelter and companionship.* And again, when it is the case that a population of individuals is no longer able to acquire and maintain their basic four needs of life without threat of loss then it will always be the case that the population will seek liberty. The population at this point no longer enjoys freedom and with the ensuing chaos the population will not strive. A population in chaos will either disband or seek liberty; regardless, a population in chaos will react as a unit.

Liberty at this point becomes the struggle between an oppressing state and a population seeking freedom. The struggle from oppression, once successful, becomes liberty. From liberty a population will institute freedom and once again strive and order has been restored.

While this endeavor is a reoccurring cycle throughout history, it nonetheless must be played out until the final solution has been achieved.

Chuck Pyburn

An Essay on Order – Economics

One of the things I've wondered about for years and years was how money made everything go and why was money that important. My minor in college was accounting and that combined with a whole bunch of self-study have come up with this essay.

The Essay

In every population there are commercial entities; hereafter referred to as companies. These companies are engaged in the commerce of goods and services; hereafter referred to as products. These products are supplied to the population in exchange for compensation; hereafter referred to as money. The collection of money by a business will be referred to as capital. As the circle of a company is now offered, the company gathers the raw materials and converts them into a product which is then exchanged with the population for money and the company continues this process to obtain capital. This sequence of events is reflective of an ordered process as it provides a product to the population.

The effort required to gather the raw materials, the conversion to a product and then providing the exchange mechanism is done by members of the population that offer their efforts in exchange for individual compensation commensurate with their contributions. It then becomes the case that as the company is able to gather capital it is able to acquire a staff of the population to accomplish the needs of the company. As this is also a necessary step it is also reflexive of order.

As the company grows it becomes able to produce various other products and offer these new products to the population in exchange for money. By diversifying a product line a company is able to survive the highs and lows of demand for a given product and able to either delete a product or add a new product as the means becomes available.

Since it will always be the case that a company has it's beginnings in a single idea of a single member of the population then it must also be the case that this individual was able to amass the necessary capital to create the company or begin the venture. This venture capital was amassed by the individual through personal efforts, or it was borrowed from other members of the population or lastly it was an investment of capital by another member, or members, of the population. Since there can only be the three cases and each case is viable, all three methods are ordered in that they provide for the basic four needs of the individual's life and his efforts to more secure those basic four needs. *The basic four needs of life are water, food, shelter and companionship.*

With regard to the venture capital, it must be the case that as the company begins its cycle of productivity that the venture capital now becomes invested capital. As capital is received from the population in exchange for the product, these monies are then applied against the amounts necessary to sustain the company, or sustainment capital. It is also the case that the received capital is also applied to the invested capital in order that, over a specific period of time, the invested capital may be retired. The remaining monies are then considered as profit above the required expenditures. The profit of the business cycle may be applied as the company sees fit. As this cycle of company startup is required it is also reflexive of order in that again, it goes toward securing the originator's basic four needs. As profit is amassed within the company it may be the case that the company may wish to invest in other startup companies and as such the cycle of business is promoted and again is reflexive of order.

Chaos may be injected into this ordered cycle at several points within the cycle and this chaos is called risk. If it is the case that the company chooses to create an inferior product then the population will reject the product and the sustainment capital will expire and the company will cease to exist. In this scenario, if there is still investment capital owing, then that investor will no longer have the means with which to recover their investment and their risk was high.

If the venture capital was insufficient to get the company into its initial productivity cycle then the product will never reach the population and the company will have failed and the venture capital is lost. The risk here was in not gathering enough venture capital and the result will be chaos.

Lastly, if the company takes profit and invest in venture capital and the venture capital is lost, as in the aforementioned manners, then the company will suffer chaos until profit margins are returned to a sustainable level. The risk to the company in this case is nominal in that the company will recover and the risk is low.

If it is the case that the company risks more than profit, in that it either pulls money from sustainment capital or it borrows money from another member of the population, then the risk is high in that it has placed the company in jeopardy if the venture fails. In this scenario, the entire process is in chaos and will only not be in chaos if it is the case that the venture has succeeded.

It could then be the case, and the worst of cases, that if a company makes a high risk investment into a company that similarly makes a high risk investment and so forth and so on and it then becomes the case that the last company invested into fails that every company before it may also fail. This chain of failure will cascade backwards until it reaches a company that made a low risk investment and then order will be restored.

It could also be the case, and the best of cases, that as one company invest in the startup of subsequent companies that each investment was low risk. This series of investments was orderly and properly thought through. With low risk investments the chances for success are great and equally of great value to the population.

Chuck Pyburn

An Essay on Order – Opportunity

Growing up as I did, I never thought of opportunity as something that came around our side of town. It wasn't until I got my first field promotion to Staff Sergeant that I began to understand the meaning of an opportunity. This essay is not what you think but it does have a good ending.

The Essay

An opportunity consists of three moving parts and a decision. Each moving part will be discussed individually as well as the decision. The offer of an opportunity is an orderly offer; however, the conduct of the opportunity is in question.

The first moving part of an opportunity is generation. An opportunity is generated by a member of the population to meet a specific requirement. This requirement can, in and of itself, be immediate or part of a planned involvement to acquire the services of another member of the population. Either way, order dictates that one member of the population is not singularly capable of providing a surplus of three of the four basic needs of life. *The basic four needs of life are water, food, shelter and companionship.* Since it will always be the case that a surplus of three of the four basic needs of life will further guarantee that and individuals basic three of four needs will not be under threat, an individual will consistently offer opportunities as they are required.

From the opportunist perspective, the second action required by an opportunity is preparedness. It will never be the case that an opportunist will be able to advantageously acquire an opportunity if the individual is not prepared to meet the opportunity. It will, therefore, always be the case that as a member of the population, an individual is constantly preparing themselves for the next available opportunity. Opportunities for the opportunist is a singular action that allows the opportunist to further secure three of their basic four needs of life without threat.

The third action in regard to an opportunity is the conduct of the opportunist if given the opportunity. This conduct will determine if the opportunity is gainful or costly. If the conduct is gainful then it must be the case that the opportunist was prepared. If the conduct is costly then it will prove that the opportunist was ill prepared and the opportunity was wasted.

Lastly is considered the decision aspect of an opportunity. It will always be the case that as an individual considers the opportunity, for whatever amount of time they may have for the consideration, that the individual will balance the current state of three of their four basic needs of life against the potential gain for those three needs of life.

It then becomes the case that opportunity is one of the higher conditions of freedom. Opportunity will only exist so long as the ability to offer opportunity and the ability to prepare for opportunity exist. When it becomes the circumstance that the state precludes the individual from offering an opportunity or precludes an individual from properly preparing for an opportunity that a specific opportunity will no longer exist.

Chuck Pyburn

An Essay on Order – Truth

As an amateur historian I've always considered the question regarding what I am reading against the truth of what I am reading. This should be a pretty cool essay.

The Essay

Truth is a simple matter of order. If it is the case that what an individual has read or heard is consistent with order then it is the truth. It will always be the case that any word, read or heard, that is not consistent with order will not be the truth. It then becomes the case, does the individual know order?

Chuck Pyburn